David,

Through this book, may you come to know the meaning and purpose for your life and why you are so valued by God and us!!

We love you,

Grandma

• Titus Chu •

BORN AGAIN

Our new life
in Christ

Born Again:
Our New Life in Christ
by Titus Chu

First Edition: September 2003
Second Edition, 2.0: January 2015
Second Edition, 2.1: July 2016,
PDF & Print on Demand

Distributed by
The Church in Cleveland Literature Service
3150 Warren Road
Cleveland, Ohio 44111

Available for purchase online.
Printed by CreateSpace,
an Amazon.com company.

Download the free PDF version of this book at
MinistryMessages.org.

Please send correspondence by email to
Notes@MinistryMessages.org.

Published by
Good Land Publishers
Ann Arbor, Michigan

Unless otherwise noted,
Scripture quotations are from the
New American Standard Bible®,
© 1960, 1995 by The Lockman Foundation.

CONTENTS

Preface

To be born again with the life of Christ is the greatest blessing any human being can ever receive. As the beginning of the Christian life, the new birth opens up an entirely new realm to those who believe in the Lord Jesus Christ. Not only are our sins forgiven, so that we are saved from God's condemnation, but in our daily, human living we are called to the full enjoyment of the salvation we have received in Christ. This includes the enjoyment of the divine, eternal life by which we were regenerated.

In this series of messages, given in 1977, Titus Chu puts together many wonderful aspects of this new birth as it is revealed in the Bible. He views the blessings we have received as being of three main categories: our new life, our new position, and our need for a new living. May this small volume enrich the understanding and experience of the new birth among so many of the Lord's children!

Study Guide & Bible Verses

To help readers get the most out of this book we also have *Born Again: The Study Guide*, and *Born Again: The Bible Verses*. *The Study Guide* helps you to review each chapter in this book, while *The Bible Verses* lists each of the verses quoted or referenced in *Born Again*, for prayer and memorization. Both may be downloaded at MinistryMessages.org.

1

What Does It Mean to Be Born Again?

The moment we first believed in the Lord Jesus and received Him as our Savior, something wonderful happened to us: we were born again. The Lord Himself speaks of this experience in John 3:3:

> *Truly, truly, I say to you, Unless one is born again, he cannot see the kingdom of God.*

To be born again is the beginning of our Christian life, for as the Lord shows us here, unless we are born again, we cannot see the kingdom of God. Yet, even though it is very common for believers today to use the term "born again," very few understand how much actually takes place at the time of our new birth.

Those who repent of their sins and open their heart to the Lord often pray something along these lines:

> *Lord Jesus, I'm a sinner. Please forgive me of my sins. I open to You now. Lord Jesus, I receive You as my Savior.*

After praying in this way, they may be so thankful and joyful that their sins are forgiven, and so grateful that they are no longer under God's judgment; these truly are great blessings that are part of the new birth. However, many believers have almost no idea that the Lord has prepared for them something much greater than simply saving them from His judgment. They don't realize that God Himself has a desire, or that He saved them for a purpose that is much higher than simply dealing with their sins.

In fact, what happened to us on the day we first believed is something so marvelous that it is almost beyond our comprehension. Only in eternity will all the riches we received in our new birth be fully revealed to us, and only then will we begin to realize what a wonder it is to be born again.

It Is Not About Going to Heaven

There are many misunderstandings about what it means to be born again. One of the first and most basic of these misunderstandings concerns where we will spend eternity. Many think that to be born again means that one day, either when we die or when the Lord comes back, we will go to heaven to live there forever; they speak of "going to heaven" as their eternal destiny. However, there is absolutely no basis in the Bible for such a belief.

God did not create man to go to heaven. Rather, He created him as an earthly being (Gen. 2:7), so that, as one made in God's image, he could exercise dominion for God over the earth (Gen. 1:26–27). As the followers of Christ today we do have a "heavenly calling" (Heb. 3:1), but this is so that we can cooperate with Him, the One who is now in heaven, to bring His heavenly kingdom down to the earth (cf. Matthew 6:9–10). At the end of the Bible we see the heavenly city, New Jerusalem, coming down out of heaven to the earth (Rev. 21:2). We are not going to heaven to live there eternally. Rather, the New Jerusalem will come down to the earth! That is where God and the believers will dwell together for eternity.

The teaching of going to heaven is not only wrong, it is profoundly misleading. The typical understanding of being born again is that we make a deal with the Lord. As a result, we will no longer go to hell, but instead we will go to heaven. Until then, we can basically live as we choose. We should go to the church of our choice, and perhaps use some of our free time to do some Christian work, but otherwise we can be very free concerning our Christian life.

Those who have such a view may think that, now that they are Christians, the Lord's concern for them is mainly to take care of their practical needs. For example, if they are short of money, they pray to the Lord for a raise. Then if their boss then gives them a raise, they pray, "Thank You, Lord, for helping me with my finances." Or, if they are late for a bus, they may pray, "Lord, please hold the bus for me." Then if they find the bus waiting for them, they tell the Lord, "Thank You for holding the bus for my sake." If they accidentally leave their wallet somewhere and go back to look for it, they pray, "Please Lord, make sure no one picks it up." Then if they find their wallet where they left it, they pray, "Lord, thank You for preventing my wallet from being stolen."

It is certainly understandable that new believers would desire the Lord's care, and it is good for us to have some basic experiences such as these. Yet, it seems that so often when Christians pray in this way, they are not looking for the Lord Himself. While the Lord often does answer such prayers, our experience of being born again should not be limited to such things.

The Need to Experience
Christ Himself

We were born again to experience Christ and gain Him. Thus, if we feel the Lord's care for us is primarily to provide for our needs while we wait to go to heaven, we are treating Him unfairly. This concept makes Him into a Santa Claus, waiting for us to pray and tell Him what we need. We assume the Lord will give us everything we ask for, but we don't seek the Lord Himself, because we don't really care about the Lord.

God does not intend that we would live according to our own choice, and His existence is not just to meet our practical needs. The greatest need we have as Christians is for Christ Himself, and the Lord's desire is to give Himself to us, so we must be very clear: we were born again to experience Christ and gain Him.

Christ Himself Now
Lives In Us

Another misunderstanding about our new birth is that when we were born again, the Holy Spirit came into us, while Christ Himself remained outside of us. Just like the thought of "going to heaven," this is also a wrong understanding which can very much frustrate and damage our Christian life.

God is triune, and very mysterious. Many Christians, according to their understanding of God, divide Him into God the Father, God the Son, and God the Spirit. Thus, they stress the fact that God is three, but neglect the oneness of the triune God.

We need to consider: when we were born again, who was the One that came into our spirit to live within us? Of course, it is true that the Holy Spirit came into us, but we should not separate the Spirit from Christ Himself. Unfortunately, some Christians seem to believe that the Spirit is inside of them as the representative of Christ, while Christ Himself is sitting on the throne in the heavens, and therefore is not inside of them. This is not the biblical view. If this were true, then being born again would have nothing to do with the person of the living Christ. We must be clear that, because God is triune, once we are born again, not only is the Spirit in us, but Christ is also in us. When we were born again, Christ Himself came to live in us.

The Bible stresses this over and over again. For example, Colossians 1:27, speaking of the saints, the believers in Christ, refers to them as those

> *to whom God willed to make known what are the riches of the glory of this mystery among the Gentiles, which is Christ in you, the hope of glory.*

According to this verse, Christ is not just on the throne in the heavens, He is also within us as the hope of glory.

Second Corinthians 13:5 says,

> *Test yourselves to see if you are in the faith; examine yourselves! Or do you not recognize this about yourselves, that Jesus Christ is in you—unless indeed you fail the test?*

This is quite serious. If Christ is not in us, then we are disapproved.

Romans 8:10 says,

> *If Christ is in you, though the body is dead because of sin, yet the spirit is life because of righteousness.*

Finally, Galatians 2:20 says,

*I have been crucified with Christ; and it is no longer
I who live, but Christ lives in me.*

These verses, along with many others, prove to us that it is not the Spirit alone who came into us when we were born again. To say the Spirit is in us merely as the representative of Christ, while Christ Himself is sitting on the throne in the heavens, is absolutely wrong. The Bible is very clear: now that we are born again, Christ Himself lives in us.

Christ's Desire for Us:
A Subjective Experience of Himself

Why is it so important to realize that Christ lives in us? Because He wants us to experience Him. To say this another way, He desires that we would know Him in an inward, subjective way, not merely in an outward, objective way. Very simply, Christ wants to be real to us in our experience! In fact, that is why He saved us.

As an illustration, suppose I have a piece of candy that I want to share with you. The taste and enjoyment of the candy is subjective, but in presenting the candy to you, I may only tell you some objective facts about it. I can tell you all the details about the piece of candy. I can tell you what it tastes like and describe its color and shape. I can talk about the ingredients, and I can tell you where I bought it. Yet, after hearing all these facts you'll finally say, "Just give me the candy! I don't care where it came from. Let me taste it!" If you take the piece of candy and put it in your mouth, it is no longer merely objective to you, it becomes subjective to you, something you have experienced.

We must ask ourselves, do we have a subjective Christ?

Yes, we know so many facts about Him, but is He real to us? We can talk about Him and appreciate Him, but do we experience Him in our daily lives? No doubt, to be born again is to have a genuine, subjective experience of Christ, but that should only be the beginning of our experience of Him. We need to substantiate our experience of being born again day after day and year after year, throughout all the rest of our life. We should enjoy the riches we received from our salvation throughout our entire life. The Lord saved us so that He could become so real to us in our experience. For this to happen, what we received the moment we first opened our heart and believed in the Lord Jesus needs to become our continuous enjoyment. This is the Lord's marvelous desire for us, and this is why we were born again.

The Three Wonderful Results of Being Born Again

Three marvelous things happened to us when we were born again. First, we received a change of life; the life of the triune God came into us and made our spirit alive. Second, we received a change of status, including a change in our position; we are no longer earthly in our nature, but are seated with Christ in the heavenly places. And because we are in Christ, we are now very different people from what we were before. Third, we received the need for a change in our living. That is, the new life within us demands that we have a new living. One aspect of this new living is that we need to come together with our fellow Christians, our fellow members of the body of Christ, to live the body life.

As we shall see throughout the remainder of this book, these were the three wonderful results of our being born again. The moment we received the Lord everything changed—our life, our status, and our living all became new.

Great in the Lord's Eyes

Because our new birth produced such a change in us, we need to realize that, the moment we were born again, we instantly became greater than all the Old Testament forefathers. God worked with many great patriarchs, kings, prophets, and scribes in the Old Testament. He appeared to them, He spoke to them, and He used them in many different and marvelous ways, but not one of them was ever born again. We appreciate Abel, Seth, Enoch, Noah, Abraham, Isaac, Jacob, Joseph, Moses, Joshua, Caleb, and so many of our forefathers. We should not look down on them, for we are their descendants by faith. Still, because none of them was ever born again, God simply could never commune with them or work with them in the way He now does with us. Nor did they receive the blessings that we enjoy today by being born again.

We may not have the assurance or the boldness to say that we are greater than all of our Old Testament forefathers, but the Lord Jesus, when He was on the earth, did have such boldness. In Matthew 11:11 He says, very directly,

Truly I say to you, among those born of women there has not arisen anyone greater than John the Baptist! Yet the one who is least in the kingdom of heaven is greater than he.

According to the Lord, John the Baptist was greater than every person who had come before Him. Of all the Old Testament saints—Abel, Enoch, Noah, Abraham, Isaac, Jacob, Moses, David, Solomon, Isaiah, Jeremiah, Daniel—not one was as great as John. Yet, the Lord also said that anyone in the kingdom of heaven is greater than John the Baptist!

We often consider ourselves to be small and insignificant, but in fact we should not look down on ourselves at all. The

Lord Jesus said that we are greater than John the Baptist, who in turn was greater than all of God's people who came before him! Even if we have only been saved a short time, we are very special to the Lord. We are greater than all of the Old Testament forefathers, and we are even greater than John the Baptist.

Praise the Lord, we have been born again! We have received a new life, a new position, and the necessity of a new living. This is why we are so great and so precious in the Lord's eyes.

Let us now go on to consider these three great matters.

2

We Have Received
the Divine Life (1)

When we believed in Jesus Christ, so many marvelous things happened to us. The first of these is that our sins were forgiven and we were cleansed from all unrighteousness. The Bible says, in Romans 3:24, that we were

justified as a gift by His grace through the redemption which is in Christ Jesus.

Ephesians 1:7 says,

In Him we have redemption through His blood, the forgiveness of our trespasses, according to the riches of His grace.

And Titus 2:14 says that Christ

gave Himself for us to redeem us from every lawless deed, and to purify for Himself a people for His own possession, zealous for good deeds.

Because we are forgiven and cleansed, God was able to do something He could not do before: He gave us a new life. As human beings, all of us have a human life, a life which is mortal, temporary, and fragile. However, the new life God gave us when we were born again is divine, eternal, and indestructible. In fact, it is the life of God Himself.

Why do we need a new life? Because, according to the Bible, before we were born again we were dead. Ephesians 2:1 says,

You were dead in your trespasses and sins.

We may not understand this, because from the standpoint of our physical life, we were very much alive. From God's point of view, however, we were dead, because we did not possess His divine, eternal life. Only the life of God is the life that is "truly life" (1 Tim. 6:19, ESV). Our human life is temporary, but the life of God is eternal. Our human life is fallen and sinful, but the life of God is divine and incorruptible. Our human life is weak and frail, but the life of God is indestructible. When we were born again, we were made alive because we received the life of God Himself. Before, we were dead in our offenses and sins, but now we are truly alive!

The Life of God

There are many verses in the Bible which reveal that we have been given a new life in Christ, and that this life is the very life of God. First John 5:12 tells us,

He who has the Son has the life; he who does not have the Son of God does not have the life.

Clearly, this verse is not speaking about the human life, but of God's divine and eternal life. If we do not have the

Son, we do not have this life. After we are born again, however, we can say, "Yes, I have the Son, so I have the life! I have the life of God Himself!"

John 3:16 is a famous verse:

For God so loved the world, that He gave His only begotten Son, that whoever believes in Him shall not perish, but have eternal life.

This verse has often been misunderstood. People feel it means that after believing in the Lord Jesus we will one day go to heaven, but this is not what it is really saying. To understand it properly, we must also read John 3:36:

He who believes in the Son has eternal life.

This verse does not say, "He who believes in the Son will one day go to heaven." Nor does it say, "He who believes in the Son will have eternal life in the next age." No! It says that once we believe in the Son, we already have eternal life. We do not have to wait until the next age. Because we are born again, we have the eternal life of God today!

In John 10:10 the Lord Jesus says,

I came that they may have life, and have it abundantly.

In this verse, the Lord tells us why He came to the earth: He came so that we could have this divine, eternal life, and even have it abundantly.

In John 14:6, the Lord says,

I am the way, and the truth, and the life; no one comes to the Father but through Me.

Here, Jesus clearly says about Himself: "I am the life."
Thus, when we believed in Christ, we received Him as our
life.

Finally, Colossians 3:4 says,

When Christ, who is our life, is revealed, then you
also will be revealed with Him in glory.

Here we see once more that, because we have been born
again, Christ is our life today. The very moment we were
born again, we received a new life, the life of God Himself.

God Himself

Yet, it was not only the life of God that came into us. We
must realize that God Himself came into us when we received His life, for the life of the triune God is inseparable
from God Himself. The triune God came into us as the eternal life (Eph. 4:6; John 14:23; 17:26; 1 Cor. 6:19). This means
that God the Father came into us, God the Son came into us,
and God the Spirit came into us. Now God is no longer
outside of us. Rather, He is within us to be our life. As Jesus
says in John 14:6, quoted above, He Himself is "the life."

A New Heart

When we were born again and received a new life, we
also received a new heart. In Ezekiel 36:26, the Lord says,

I will give you a new heart and put a new spirit within
you; and I will remove the heart of stone from your
flesh and give you a heart of flesh.

We must realize that before we were born again, our spirit was dead, and our heart was like a stone in relation to the things of God. But after we were born again, we received a new heart. This new heart is called a "heart of flesh." It is a heart that is tender and sensitive, and it is full of feeling towards God.

People who are not born again are often hard towards the things of God. That is, their heart is stony, because their spirit is dead. For example, some say, "Where is God? If you can't show me God, then I will not believe in Him." This is nonsensical. We don't need to see everything in order for it to exist. No one can say, "Show me the air. If you can't show me the air, then I won't believe it exists." We can't see the air, but if we stop breathing we will die.

If someone tells us, "I won't believe in God unless you show me God," we should simply reply, "I don't have to show you God. If you just call on the Lord's name, then you will have Him as your life. If you refuse to believe in the Lord, you will remain in death. You may be alive as a human being, but your spirit is dead to God. Because your spirit is dead, your heart is as hard as stone. That is why you question God's existence."

People who have a stony heart always think that they are right and everyone else is wrong. They do their best to profit at the expense of others. They are centered on themselves and have no interest in the things of God. However, we should not condemn those who are like this, for before we believed in the Lord, we also had such a stony heart. It was only when we were born again that God gave us a new heart so that we could respond to His life within us. Once we believed, our heart became a heart of flesh, one which was soft and tender towards God and sensitive to the new life we had been given.

A New Spirit

In addition to speaking of our new heart, Ezekiel 36:26 says that God gave us a new spirit when we were born again. When God first created man, He created him with a human spirit to contact God, but due to the fall the spirit within man became deadened. However, once we are born again we can say, "My spirit is living!" This is because we have received a new spirit, a spirit filled with life. Before we believed in the Lord Jesus, our human spirit was dead. But now we have a new spirit, a living spirit.

Before we were born again, whenever we heard about Jesus we were very bothered. Whenever we went to a church service we felt it was too long, and whenever we saw a Bible we wanted to toss it aside. When we were born again, however, we received a new spirit, and suddenly everything changed. We began to enjoy meeting with Christians, we loved reading the Bible, and we loved hearing and talking about Jesus. Because our spirit was made alive, we became so responsive to the things related to God. This is the result of being born again.

The Light of Life

John 1:4 tells us, concerning the Lord Jesus,

In Him was life, and the life was the Light of men.

Then the Lord Himself says, in John 8:12,

I am the Light of the world; he who follows Me will not walk in the darkness, but will have the Light of life.

This means that, by receiving the life of God, we also received the Light of life.

We know from our own experience that before we were born again, we were in darkness. We didn't know who God was or if He even existed. We didn't know the meaning or the purpose of our own human life. We didn't even know right from wrong, and we didn't really care. When we were born again, however, we received the Light of life, because the new life we received enlightened us. As a result, God became real to us, and our existence became meaningful.

This light also exposed the darkness within us. We began to realize what was right and what was wrong. We even learned that some things were wrong even though they appeared to be fine. Concerning many things, the Light of life made us realize, "I can't do this anymore. It used to seem fine, and it seems normal outwardly, but I just sense that God is not pleased with it." Today, the Light of life constantly shines within us and enlightens us.

The Law of Life

When we were born again we also received the law of life. Romans 8:2 says,

The law of the Spirit of life in Christ Jesus has set you free from the law of sin and of death.

What is the law of life? Every kind of life—whether it be vegetable life, animal life, or human life—has its law. For example, our human life demands sleep. If we don't get enough sleep over a long period of time, we easily become irritable. This does not mean we are evil. We simply need to get more sleep, and once we do, everything will be fine. We have to fulfill the law of our human life.

Now that we are born again, we have the life of God. That means that within us, in addition to the law of our human life, there is now another law: the law of the divine life. As a result, something strange happens to us: we find that we are limited and restricted within, so that now there are many things we simply cannot do.

For example, before, if we were driving in our car and another driver cut us off, we would be tempted to react. We might have even cut him off in return. Now that we are born again, however, we are no longer so free. If someone cuts us off while we are driving and we are about to react, immediately something within us says, "No, I'm not happy with you reacting like that! Don't do that!" The law of life within us disagrees with anything that does not correspond to God Himself. This is why the more we do things that are according to the life of God, the happier we become. The more we learn to live by the law of life, the more we sense the Lord's presence.

Conclusion

We received so much the moment we were born again! We will probably never fully comprehend it. When we first opened to the Lord and received Him as our Savior, the triune God entered into us to be our very life, and at that moment we received a new life with so many wonderful items. We received a new heart and a new spirit. We received the Light of life, the law of life, and much, much more. We treasure what the Lord has done for us and all the riches He has given to us. All of these items are for us to enjoy now, because we have been born again. Praise the Lord!

3

We Have Received the Divine Life (2)

In this chapter we will cover an additional four points on the marvelous life we received when we were born again, and also consider the way this life comes into our being.

The Spirit as a Seal

Ephesians 1:13 says,

In Him, you also, after listening to the message of truth, the gospel of your salvation—having also believed, you were sealed in Him with the Holy Spirit of promise.

This verse tells us that we were "sealed with the Holy Spirit." If you own a book, you might mark it with a seal so that everyone knows it belongs to you. When we believed, the Lord marked us with His seal, the seal of the Holy Spirit. From that moment all could see that we belong to Him.

When Christians are first born again, they are often told to give themselves to the Lord. In reality, however, such exhortations are not necessary, for if we are saved, it means the Lord has sealed us, and we already belong to Him. Because we have been sealed with the Holy Spirit, we will be encouraged and strengthened to live for the Lord by the divine life within us. It is no longer possible for us to belong to someone else. In fact, we cannot even belong to ourselves, for the life within us will always remind us that we belong to the Lord. Second Timothy 2:19 tells us,

The firm foundation of God stands, having this seal, "The Lord knows those who are His."

Before we were born again, we may have thought that we belonged to ourselves, but actually, we were in bondage to Satan. Now, however, we have been sealed with the Holy Spirit, and we are the Lord's possession. If Satan were to come and try to take us away from the Lord, the Lord would say, "Don't touch him! He belongs to Me." The moment we opened our heart and the Lord came into us, at that very moment we were sealed. The seal of the Holy Spirit testifies that now we belong to God Himself.

The Spirit as a Pledge

Not only were we sealed by the Spirit, but we also received the pledge of the Spirit. Ephesians 1:13–14 says,

The Holy Spirit...is given as a pledge of our inheritance, with a view to the redemption of God's own possession, to the praise of His glory.

And 2 Corinthians 1:21–22 tells us,

God...sealed us and gave us the Spirit in our hearts as a pledge.

What is the difference between being sealed with the Holy Spirit and having the Spirit as a pledge? For us to be sealed means that we belong to God, while for us to receive the Spirit as a pledge means that God belongs to us.

The word "pledge" in this verse can also be translated as "foretaste" or "guarantee." The Spirit as a pledge is actually a foretaste, a guarantee, of our enjoyment in eternity. Therefore, we do not have to imagine what things will be like in eternity, because we already have a foretaste of it! Often when we are enjoying the Lord, especially when we are with other believers, we experience an incredible joy, which is a foretaste of our eternal joy. Thus, if someone asks us, "What will it be like in eternity?" we should say, "Have you ever enjoyed the Lord in your spirit with the other believers? That is the foretaste of our enjoyment in the age to come." Whenever we enjoy the Lord in our spirit, we get excited. We realize, "Hallelujah! I have the Lord's presence. Oh, it is so good! It is so wonderful!"

This is the foretaste that the Lord has given to us. Our foretaste today helps us to realize that in eternity we will be joyful and satisfied, but still we must realize that it is only a foretaste. Our enjoyment in eternity will be even richer, higher, and fuller than what we are experiencing now.

The Anointing

When we were born again, we also received what the Bible calls "the anointing." First John 2:27 says,

As for you, the anointing which you received from Him abides in you, and you have no need for anyone to teach you; but as His anointing teaches you about all things, and is true and is not a lie, and just as it has taught you, you abide in Him.

The word "anointing" in this verse is a gerund, a verbal noun, which means it is something active. Ever since we were born again, the life of God has been moving within us all the time, and this moving of the divine life within us is the anointing.

According to this verse, the anointing simply teaches us to abide in Him. To follow the Lord after we are born again is not to live by mere doctrinal teachings, but to experience Him within us, through the anointing. This anointing teaches us how to abide in Him. In fact, not only does it teach us, but it also anoints the essence of God Himself into us. When we were born again, we received the very life of God. Now the anointing works the essence of that life with all the riches of God into our being. The more we experience the anointing, the more God Himself is worked into us.

How God Comes Into Us: As the Life-giving Spirit

We have already seen that when we were born again, God Himself came into us as life. Yet, we might ask, how does He come into us? The answer is, He comes into us as the life-giving Spirit, in resurrection. We see this in 1 Corinthians 15:45, which states, concerning the resurrection of Christ,

It is written, "The first man, Adam, became a living soul." The last Adam became a life-giving spirit.

This verse tells us that, through His death and resurrection, the man Jesus Christ, "the last Adam," became "a life-giving Spirit." This is truly mysterious, for it touches on the matter of the Trinity. Since early in the church age, orthodox Christians have understood that within the trinity of the Godhead, the Father, Son, and Spirit are always distinct, but never separate. This verse is referring to the Son in His humanity—the last Adam—and reminds us that the Son joined Himself to the race of Adam in incarnation. Then, in His death on the cross as the "last Adam," Christ brought an end to Adam's race before God (cf. Rom. 6:3–4). Finally, through His resurrection, His human nature was uplifted and glorified with the divine life, so that now He is a glorified God-man.

As a result of going through such a process, Jesus Christ became the "life-giving Spirit" (cf. John 6:63; 2 Cor. 3:17–18). This glorified, exalted Lord is the Spirit who gives life. That is, He can now impart to His fellow human beings the divine life that has been in Him, as God, from the very beginning (John 1:4; cf. 10:10; 11:25; 12:24). This is what it means to say that "the last Adam became a life-giving Spirit." When we were born again, we received Christ as the life-giving Spirit.

There are several additional verses that relate to this matter. John 7:37–39 says,

> Now on the last day, the great day of the feast, Jesus stood and cried out, saying, "If anyone is thirsty, let him come to Me and drink. He who believes in Me, as the Scripture said, 'From his innermost being will flow rivers of living water.'" But this He spoke of the Spirit, whom those who believed in Him were to receive; for the Spirit was not yet given, because Jesus was not yet glorified.

Here we again see that it was not until after Jesus was resurrected that God could come into us as the Spirit to be our life within.

Christ also spoke to the disciples of the Spirit coming after the resurrection in John 14:16–17:

I will ask the Father, and He will give you another Helper, that He may be with you forever; that is the Spirit of truth, whom the world cannot receive, because it does not see Him or know Him, but you know Him because He abides with you and will be in you.

And He says in John 16:13,

But when He, the Spirit of truth, comes, He will guide you into all the truth.

Christ as the life-giving Spirit has come into our human spirit and will guide us into all the truth, or reality, of what we have received.

How We Touch God's Life: In Our Human Spirit

It is very important for us to realize that, because God comes to us as the Spirit, we can only experience the life of God by touching the Spirit within our human spirit. Romans 8:16 says,

The Spirit Himself testifies with our spirit that we are children of God.

The Spirit brings us into all the reality of what we received when we were born again. Before we were born again, God was objective, theoretical, and untouchable to us. We did not know God and could not see God, for God cannot be seen with human eyes. Once we believed in Him, however, we received the Spirit, and God became very real and subjective to us. As those who are born again, we can now experience God in our human spirit!

The function of the life-giving Spirit is to impart God's life into us. Whenever we exercise our human spirit, the life-giving Spirit begins to operate, and the more He operates, the more we partake of the riches of God's life within us. It is only because God is the Spirit and life that He is able to come and live within us. He is the infinite God, the One who created the whole universe. He states in Isaiah 66:1,

Heaven is My throne
* and the earth is My footstool.*
Where then is a house you could build for Me?
And where is a place that I may rest?

Yet, where is this great God today? He is not only filling the heavens and the earth; He is also dwelling within us! (John 17:25; 1 Cor. 6:17, 19). Do we realize that God is within our human spirit as life to be enjoyed and received by us? According to our concept, we may feel that God is too great to be within us, but according to the Bible the great Creator does indeed live in us today. In resurrection the Lord Jesus became the life-giving Spirit, and now He lives in our spirit and imparts God as life to us. Now we can say, "God lives inside of me! He is in my human spirit!" He is there as the life-giving Spirit, imparting His life and all His riches to us. As the Spirit, He will bring us into all the reality of what we received when we were born again.

Conclusion

At the time of our new birth, we were sealed with the Holy Spirit, and we received the Spirit as a pledge; Hallelujah! Now the life of God is moving within us as the anointing, and the life-giving Spirit is bringing us into all the reality of this wonderful new life in us. Again we say: Hallelujah!

4

Our Position Before
We Were Born Again

In the previous chapters, we considered the new life we received when we were born again. Now we need to see that, when we were born again, we also received a new position. Colossians 1:13 tells us,

> *He rescued us from the domain of darkness, and transferred us to the kingdom of His beloved Son.*

According to this verse, before we were saved we were in one place, the domain of darkness, but now we have been transferred into another place, the kingdom of God's beloved Son. What a marvelous change is this! In order to fully appreciate our new position, however, we must first be clear about the position we left behind, so in this chapter we will look at the different aspects of the negative position we were in before we were born again.

In Darkness

Before we were born again, we were blind to the things of God and even to the purpose of our own human life. We didn't know whether God truly existed, we didn't know that we needed a Savior, and our human life was empty and meaningless. If brief, we were just in darkness. When Paul was brought before King Agrippa, he testified that the Lord had appeared to him and commissioned him to preach the gospel. He said, in Acts 26:18, that the Lord had told him he was being sent to the Gentiles

to open their eyes so that they may turn from darkness to light and from the dominion of Satan to God.

The apostle Peter, in 1 Peter 2:9, also speaks of this transfer, when he tells us that the Lord has called us

out of darkness into His marvelous light.

These are wonderful verses, in that they tell us we have been called into God's light. However, they also show us that before we were born again, we were in a position of darkness. Thank the Lord, we have now been delivered from the domain of darkness.

Under the Authority of Satan

Before we were born again, we were under the authority of Satan, God's enemy. According to the Bible, Satan has a kingdom on this earth. In Matthew 12:26, Jesus says,

If Satan casts out Satan, he is divided against himself; how then will his kingdom stand?

All those who have not been born again are in Satan's kingdom and under his authority. That is the reason why Paul was commissioned by the Lord to turn people from "the dominion of Satan to God."

Of course, everyone likes to think that they belong to themselves and are under their own authority. They believe that they can live their own lives on their own terms. According to the Bible, however, no one is under his own authority. Everyone is in either the kingdom of Satan or the kingdom of God. If you are born again, you have entered God's kingdom and have been brought under God's authority, but if you are not born again, then you are under Satan's authority. You may think that you are your own master, but actually you are in Satan's kingdom. This is true no matter who you are, where you live, or what you do. Every human being who does not believe in the Lord Jesus is under the authority of Satan. This was also our position before we were born again.

In Sin

Before we were born again, we were in sin. Romans 3:23 says,

All have sinned and fall short of the glory of God.

This is true of every human being. Romans 3:10 says,

As it is written, "There is none righteous, not even one."

In our former position, we may have had no feeling about the many things we did that were unrighteous. We offended God all the time, even though we may not have realized it. We not only committed sins, but we were dwelling in sin and abiding in sin. Our entire life was just in sin.

In Death

The Bible also tells us that before we were born again, we were in death. Sin and death are closely related. Romans 5:12 says,

> *Through one man sin entered into the world, and death through sin, and so death spread to all men, because all sinned.*

Because we were in sin, we were also in death. To say that we were in death, spiritually speaking, means that we had no feeling towards God. That is why Ephesians 2:1 says,

> *You were dead in your trespasses and sins.*

In the eyes of the world we may have been very busy, doing many things. Because our spirit was dead, however, we had no feeling towards God in our human spirit. Thus, in the eyes of God we were like a walking corpse. We didn't know where we came from or where we were going. God seemed far away from us. Only after we were born again did we realize, "All of my life I was actually dead. I thought I was alive all these years, but I was abiding in death. I had no feeling towards God at all until now." This proves that before we were born again, we were in death.

Under God's Judgment

Before we were born again we were under God's judgment. Romans 3:19 says,

Now we know that whatever the Law says, it speaks to those who are under the Law, so that every mouth may be closed and all the world may become accountable to God.

The reason God gave the Law in the Old Testament was to bring the whole world under His judgment. It was only possible for man to know his true condition because God gave him the Law. By giving the Law, God was saying to mankind, "It matters to Me what you do! I did not create human beings to be so sinful and so fallen as you are!"

To some people, it may not matter whether they are in God's kingdom or not, but it certainly does matter to God. Thus, He gave the Law to expose man's sinful and unrighteous condition and to bring the world under His judgment. Before we were born again we were, like all other unsaved human beings, under God's righteous judgment.

Under God's Condemnation

Not only were we under God's judgment, but we were also condemned. To be condemned is both to be found guilty and to be completely disapproved. God's judgment on us resulted in our condemnation. John 3:18 (NKJV) says,

He who believes in Him is not condemned; but he who does not believe is condemned already, because he has not believed in the name of the only begotten Son of God.

Because we did not believe in the name of the only begotten Son of God, we were under God's condemnation.

Slaves to Impurity and Lawlessness

The Bible also tells us that before we were born again, we were slaves to impurity and lawlessness. Romans 6:19 says,

I am speaking in human terms because of the weakness of your flesh. For just as you presented your members as slaves to impurity and to lawlessness, resulting in further lawlessness, so now present your members as slaves to righteousness, resulting in sanctification.

Before we knew the Lord, we were just slaves to impurity and lawlessness. We had no way to free ourselves, even though we may have tried many times, and even made up our mind to change. There were things about ourselves that we knew were wrong, and we decided, "I'm not going to do those things anymore." Nonetheless, there was a power within us that enslaved us to those unclean things, and we found that in ourselves we had no ability to change. This shows us that, as the Bible says, we were slaves to impurity and lawlessness. This was part of our hopeless position before we were born again.

Children of Wrath and Sons of Disobedience

Finally, before we were born again we were children of wrath and sons of disobedience. Ephesians 2:1–3 says,

You were dead in your trespasses and sins, in which you formerly walked according to the course of this world, according to the prince of the power of the air, of the spirit that is now working in the sons of

disobedience. Among them we too all formerly lived in the lusts of our flesh, indulging the desires of the flesh and of the mind, and were by nature children of wrath, even as the rest.

And John 3:36 says,

He who believes in the Son has eternal life; but he who does not obey the Son will not see life, but the wrath of God abides on him.

Who were we before we were born again? We were just children of wrath and sons of disobedience, those who disobeyed the Son. This was our nature and position by birth. Even when we were young, we had a tendency towards disobedience. We were disobedient to our parents and disobedient to our teachers. Then when we grew up, we were disobedient to God Himself. Before we believed in the Lord, we often reacted when someone talked about Jesus. We could talk about philosophy and religion in a general way, but if someone said, "You need to believe in Jesus," we would say, "I'm not interested!" Because we were disobedient to the Son, refusing to believe in Him and be saved, we were under God's wrath.

Transferred into a New Position

From all of these points we can see that, formerly, we were poor, hopeless sinners, and as such we were in a miserable and desperate position. Now, however, we have nothing to do with where we were before, because God has transferred us into an entirely new position. Now that we are born again, we are no longer in darkness, we are no longer under the authority of Satan, we are no longer in sin, we are no longer in death, we are no longer under God's judgment, we are no longer condemned, we are no longer slaves to impurity and lawlessness, and we are no longer children of wrath and sons of disobedience. Hallelujah, now we have nothing to do with where we were before! By being born again, we have been transferred out of our former position.

5

Our Wonderful
New Position

As we have seen, Colossians 1:13 tells us of something
wonderful that God has done on our behalf. It says,

> *He rescued us from the domain of darkness, and
> transferred us to the kingdom of His beloved Son.*

Before we were saved our position was truly hopeless
and miserable. We were in darkness, we were under the authority of Satan, we were in sin, and we were in death. We
were under God's judgment and therefore condemned. We
were slaves to impurity and lawlessness, and we were children of wrath and sons of disobedience. As fallen and sinful
human beings, we needed a change in our position. Now, as
those who are born again, we have been delivered from our
old position and all the negative things related to it, and transferred into a wonderful new position. Praise the Lord!

It is crucial for us to see that we have received a new position in Christ, because the kind of living we have will be
determined by the position we have. Being born again is like
migrating from an impoverished country, where there is no
hope, to a rich and prosperous country, one with unlimited
hope for the future. Spiritually speaking, we are now in a

new "country," a new kingdom with so many riches. We have migrated from the kingdom of Satan to the kingdom of God, and now in our new position, we can enjoy all the marvelous riches that God has prepared for us.

In this chapter we will cover several aspects of the wonderful new position we have now that we've been born again. Then in the next chapter we will go on to consider what we have become now that we are in Christ.

No Longer Condemned

The very first item in our new position as believers in Christ is that we are no longer condemned. Our old position was indeed one of condemnation, but in our new position we are free from condemnation. John 3:18 (ESV) tells us that those who do not believe are already condemned, but this verse also says,

Whoever believes in Him is not condemned.

And Romans 8:1 tells us,

There is now no condemnation for those who are in Christ Jesus.

Justified

After being born again, we are justified. To be justified means that God approves us according to the standard of His righteousness. Formerly, we were in sin and therefore under God's righteous judgment, but now we are acceptable to God because we have believed in Christ and thus received His redemption. Romans 3:24 says we are *justified as a gift by His grace through the redemption which is in Christ Jesus.*

Romans 5:1 says,

Therefore, having been justified by faith, we have peace with God through our Lord Jesus Christ.

And Romans 8:33 says,

Who will bring a charge against God's elect? God is the one who justifies.

Because we are born again, God declares that we are righteous. This is based entirely on the death of Christ. By believing in the Lord Jesus, we are justified.

Delivered from the Authority of Darkness

According to Acts 26:18, as mentioned above, the Lord sent the apostle Paul to the Gentiles

to open their eyes so that they may turn from darkness to light and from the dominion of Satan to God.

This shows us that before we were in Satan's kingdom and under the authority of darkness, but now we have been brought into the kingdom of God's beloved Son. Praise Him!

Joined to the Lord

In our new position, we are joined to the Lord. First Corinthians 6:17 says,

*The one who joins himself to the Lord is one spirit
with Him.*

To understand this statement we need to consider some
related verses. According to John 3:6, it was in our human
spirit that we were born of the Spirit of God:

*That which is born of the flesh is flesh, and that which
is born of the Spirit is spirit.*

Second Corinthians 3:17 tells us the Lord Jesus is the Spirit:

*Now the Lord is the Spirit, and where the Spirit of
the Lord is, there is liberty.*

When we put these verses together, we see that once we
are born again, the Lord as the Spirit is one with our human
spirit, which is the deepest part of our being. Thus, to say we
are "joined to the Lord" and "one spirit with Him" means
that after being born again, we are joined to the Lord in our
human spirit. This is also seen in Romans 8:16, which says,

*The Spirit Himself testifies with our spirit that we
are children of God.*

Where does the Spirit of God testify? In our human spirit.

In the Triune God

The next several points concern what we are in now that
we have been born again.

First, we are in the triune God. When the Lord Jesus was
still on the earth, He prayed to the Father for His believers,
in John 17:21, asking

that they may all be one; even as You, Father, are in
Me and I in You, that they also may be in Us, so that
the world may believe that You sent Me.

The Lord prayed for us to be in the triune God, and this
has now been accomplished. We know this from Colossians
3:3, which tells us,

You have died and your life is hidden with Christ in
God.

Once we are born again we are in the triune God.

In Life

As we have seen, before being born again, we were in
death. Ephesians 2:1 says,

You were dead in your trespasses and sins.

But when we were born again, we were made alive. Therefore, Ephesians 2:3–5 goes on to tell us,

Among [the unbelievers we] all formerly lived in the
lusts of our flesh, indulging the desires of the flesh
and of the mind, and were by nature children of wrath,
even as the rest. But God, being rich in mercy, be-
cause of His great love with which He loved us, even
when we were dead in our transgressions, made us
alive together with Christ.

Here we see that, whereas before we lived a fleshly life
and were under God's condemnation, we are now in a position of life.

John 5:24 also tells us that we are now in life:

Truly, truly, I say to you, he who hears My word, and believes Him who sent Me, has eternal life, and does not come into judgment, but has passed out of death into life.

Thank the Lord, we have "passed out of death into life!"

In Light

Before we were born again we were in darkness, but now we are in the light. First Peter 2:9 says,

You are a chosen race, a royal priesthood, a holy nation, a people for God's own possession, so that you may proclaim the excellencies of Him who has called you out of darkness into His marvelous light.

Ephesians 5:8 says,

You were formerly darkness, but now you are Light in the Lord; walk as children of Light.

And Colossians 1:12 tells us that we should give thanks to the Father,

who has qualified us to share in the inheritance of the saints in Light.

As those who are born again, we are "the saints in Light."

In Grace

Formerly, we were in sin and therefore under the law, but now that we are born again, we are in grace. Romans 5:2 says,

> *Through [Jesus Christ] we have obtained our intro-duction by faith into this grace in which we stand; and we exult in hope of the glory of God.*

And Romans 5:20–21 says,

> *The Law came in so that the transgression would in-crease; but where sin increased, grace abounded all the more, so that, as sin reigned in death, even so grace would reign through righteousness to eternal life through Jesus Christ our Lord.*

Because we are now in the triune God, we are also stand-ing in grace, which is really the triune God enjoyed by us.

In Hope

Before we were born again, we had no hope, and were without God. Ephesians 2:12 speaks of this fact:

> *Remember that you were at that time separate from Christ, excluded from the commonwealth of Israel, and strangers to the covenants of promise, having no hope and without God in the world.*

However, Romans 8:24 (Darby) tells us that we were "saved in hope." In addition, 1 Peter 1:3 says,

Blessed be the God and Father of our Lord Jesus Christ, who according to His great mercy has caused us to be born again to a living hope through the resurrection of Jesus Christ from the dead.

According to this verse, we are "born again to a living hope."

In Resurrection

The fact that we were formerly in death, but are now in life, means that we are now in resurrection. Ephesians 2:4–6 says,

God, being rich in mercy, because of His great love with which He loved us, even when we were dead in our transgressions, made us alive together with Christ (by grace you have been saved), and raised us up with Him, and seated us with Him in the heavenly places in Christ Jesus.

And Colossians 3:1 tells us,

If you have been raised up with Christ, keep seeking the things above, where Christ is, seated at the right hand of God.

When we were born again, we became one with the resurrected Christ. This means that when the Lord Jesus was raised from the dead, we were also raised with Him. Just as the Lord has passed out of death into life, so we also are in resurrection.

In the Heavenlies

By being born again, we have been seated in Christ Jesus in the heavenlies, the highest place in the universe. This is because we are one with Christ not only in His resurrection, but also in His ascension. Many Christians are waiting to go to heaven, but the Bible tells us we have already been seated in the heavenly places with Christ! Ephesians 2:6 tells us,

[God] raised us up with Him, and seated us with Him in the heavenly places in Christ Jesus.

It is in this new position that we receive every spiritual blessing, as referred to in Ephesians 1:3:

Blessed be the God and Father of our Lord Jesus Christ, who has blessed us with every spiritual blessing in the heavenly places in Christ.

Thus, according to the Bible, we do not have to wait to go to heaven, for we have already been seated there with Christ! And in our new position in the heavenlies, we have been blessed with every spiritual blessing in Him.

In the Kingdom of the Son of God's Love

By being born again, we entered into a new kingdom. As we have already seen, God transferred us into "the kingdom of His beloved Son" when we believed (Col. 1:13). We have left the dark, satanic kingdom behind, and our wonderful new position is in the kingdom of the Son of God's love.

Set Free from Sin

By being born again, we are set free from sin. Romans 6:18 says,

Having been freed from sin, you became slaves of righteousness.

And we see in Romans 6:20 and 22,

When you were slaves of sin, you were free in regard to righteousness....But now having been freed from sin and enslaved to God, you derive your benefit, resulting in sanctification, and the outcome, eternal life.

Formerly we were slaves of sin, but after being born again we are set free from sin. This means that sin cannot bother us anymore. We should remember this whenever Satan comes to accuse us. Whenever we hear the enemy say, "You claim to be a Christian, but look at what you just did!" we can simply reply, "The Lord has set me free from sin!"

This should be our answer to any of the enemy's accusations. Satan wants us to be occupied with our sin, but we should not accept his accusations, because the Bible tells us that we are now free from sin.

Set Free from Death

Formerly we were in death, but by being born again we are set free from death. Romans 8:2 says,

The law of the Spirit of life in Christ Jesus has set you free from the law of sin and death.

Before we were born again, we lived under the power of death. The prospect of physical death caused us to fear (Heb. 2:15), and the death element within us caused us to live a life according to the prince of this world, Satan. In brief, we had death within and death without. However, in His wonderful death on the cross, Christ destroyed Satan. Moreover, through His resurrection, Christ became the life-giving Spirit, who gave us eternal life the moment we believed. As a result, we now enjoy "the law of the Spirit of life" (Rom. 8:2). We are released from the law of sin and death by being in Christ Jesus.

Set Free from the World

We have also been set free from the world. The Bible tells us that the world is Satan's kingdom. According to 1 John 5:19,

We know that we are of God, and that the whole world lies in the power of the evil one.

The Bible also tells us that Satan is "the ruler of this world" (John 16:11). Before being born again we were a part of Satan's kingdom, the world, but by believing in the Lord Jesus, we have been set free from the world. Galatians 6:14 says,

May it never be that I would boast, except in the cross of our Lord Jesus Christ, through which the world has been crucified to me, and I to the world.

Set Free from the Flesh

As we have already seen, before being born again we "lived in the lusts of our flesh, indulging the desires of the flesh and of the mind" (Eph. 2:3). But in our new position we are free from our flesh, so that it can no longer bind us. Galatians 5:24 says,

Those who belong to Christ Jesus have crucified the flesh with its passions and desires.

Set Free from
the Authority of Satan

The freedom we have in Christ includes being freed from Satan's authority and brought into the kingdom of God (Col. 1:13). How does God accomplish this transfer? He does it by making us alive. Ephesians 2:4–5 says,

God, being rich in mercy, because of His great love with which He loved us, even when we were dead in our transgressions, made us alive together with Christ (by grace you have been saved).

From all of these points, we can see that we have been set free from five negative things: sin, death, the world, the flesh, and the authority of Satan.

Slaves of Righteousness

When we were born again, we were set free, yet at the same time we became slaves. Romans 6:18 says,

Having been freed from sin, you became slaves of righteousness.

To be enslaved means that we have no choice. Even when we try to be unrighteous, something within us compels us to be righteous. This shows us that now we are slaves of righteousness.

Slaves to God

Even more wonderful than being a slave of righteousness is being a slave to God. To see this we can refer again to Romans 6:22, which says,

Now having been freed from sin and enslaved to God, you derive your benefit, resulting in sanctification, and the outcome, eternal life.

We have been set free from sin, death, the world, the flesh, and the authority of Satan, and now we are enslaved to God!

Peace with God

In our new position, we have peace with God. Romans 5:1 says,

Therefore, having been justified by faith, we have peace with God through our Lord Jesus Christ.

The fact that we have peace with God means that we shouldn't be bothered by our personal condition anymore. We shouldn't say, "I'm so poor. I'm so defeated. I have so many failures." The Bible makes it clear that we have peace with God already. God doesn't remember those things, so why should we bother to remember them? Why should we look at our failures? God says, "I don't see them," and we should say, "I don't see them either." Our Christian life should not be one that is under condemnation, but rather, one of peace and rest. Now that we are born again, we have peace with God. Praise Him!

6

What We Have Become in Christ

In this chapter we cover what we have become in Christ, now that we have our new position in Him.

Vessels unto Honor

According to the Bible, every human being is a vessel. Romans 9:21 says,

> *Does not the potter have a right over the clay, to make from the same lump one vessel for honorable use and another for common use?*

Now that we are saved, we have become vessels unto honor, because as vessels we contain God's divine life. Second Corinthians 4:7 says,

> *We have this treasure in earthen vessels, so that the surpassing greatness of the power will be of God and not from ourselves.*

As human beings, we are earthen vessels, but when we were born again we received a heavenly treasure into our earthen vessels. We became vessels unto honor, because we received the very life of God Himself. As vessels we are still earthen, but now we contain something that is truly heavenly. We do not need to dream about "going to heaven" one day, because we already have something heavenly within us. This content, the life of God, makes us vessels unto honor.

The Temple of God

We have become vessels unto honor, and our bodies have become temples of the Holy Spirit. In 1 Corinthians 6:19 the apostle Paul asks,

Do you not know that your body is a temple of the Holy Spirit who is in you, whom you have from God, and that you are not your own?

Individually, each of our bodies is a temple. Together, according to 1 Corinthians 3:16, we are the temple of God, for in this verse Paul asks,

Do you not know that you are a temple of God and that the Spirit of God dwells in you?

It is important to note that the "you" in this verse is plural in the original Greek. Therefore, this verse is saying that all the saints are, together, a temple of God. We can also see this in 2 Corinthians 6:16, which says,

We are the temple of the living God; just as God said, "I will dwell in them and walk among them; And I will be their God, and they shall be My people."

In the Old Testament age God's temple was a physical building in Jerusalem, but in the New Testament age God's people themselves are His temple. We as believers are now the temple of God, and the Spirit of God dwells in us and abides in us. All of us together, by being born again, have become the temple of God.

The Members of Christ

We have also become the members of Christ, as the members of His body. There are several verses which tell us this. Romans 12:5 says,

We, who are many, are one body in Christ, and individually members one of another.

First Corinthians 6:15 says,

Do you not know that your bodies are members of Christ?

First Corinthians 12:12 says,

Even as the body is one and yet has many members, and all the members of the body, though they are many, are one body, so also is Christ.

And Ephesians 5:29–30 says,

No one ever hated his own flesh, but nourishes and cherishes it, just as Christ also does the church, because we are members of His body.

We are now members of the body of Christ, which means that we are members of Christ Himself. However, before we were saved, all of us were taught to be individualistic, and this affects our understanding of salvation. When we first prayed to the Lord to receive Him, we assumed that our salvation was for ourselves. We certainly didn't have any thought that our salvation was for Christ, or that the Lord would tell us, "You were saved to be a member of My body." After being born again, we may have the concept that we can still live in an individualistic way, but the verses above show us that we have been born again to be members of Christ's body.

We should not think, "As long as I take good care of myself spiritually and pray from time to time, that's enough. I can live the Christian life on my own." That is a fallen concept. The Lord would respond, "No, that is not My way. That is not why I saved you. You were born again to be a member of My body. You were saved as an individual, but you have received a corporate life, and I have placed you in a corporate position. You cannot live as an individual any longer." By being born again we have become the members of Christ. Our new position does not allow us to be individualistic anymore.

Fellow Citizens with the Saints

We have already seen that we have been transferred into God's kingdom. Now we need to realize that we have many fellow citizens with us in God's kingdom, namely, our fellow believers in Christ. Ephesians 2:19 says,

You are no longer strangers and aliens, but you are fellow citizens with the saints, and are of God's household.

Because we are all in the same kingdom, we all share the same citizenship. All who believe in the Lord Jesus are "fellow citizens." This shows us again that our new position is a corporate one. It is foolish to think that we can be individualistic after we are born again. In our new position, we are fellow citizens with the saints in the kingdom of God.

Members of the Household of God

Ephesians 2:19 also tells us that when we were born again, we were born into God's household. The word "household" in this verse can also be translated as "family," which means that we have become members of the family of God. This shows us, once again, that we can no longer be by ourselves. We should not think, "I'll just take care of my own spiritual condition," for God wants us to be with all the other members of His family. We were born again not only to be individual vessels, but also to be God's temple, to be members of the body of Christ, and to be fellow citizens with the saints and members of the household of God. Since this is the case, how could we choose to be isolated or to remain by ourselves? How could we try to have an individualistic Christian life? We must realize that our Christian life is a corporate matter, in which we are the members of God's household, His very family.

God's Masterpiece

Ephesians 2:10 tells us,

We are His workmanship, created in Christ Jesus for good works, which God prepared beforehand so that we would walk in them.

The word "workmanship" in this verse can also be translated "masterpiece." We are now God's masterpiece, God's workmanship. However, this does not mean that the work is complete once we are born again. Rather, for us to become God's masterpiece requires God to work on us continually, all the rest of our lives. After we are born again, God often comes in to "cut" and "hammer" us. He works on us and adjusts us, according to our measure of growth in the divine life, to transform us into the image of Christ. Now that we are born again, we are in the proper position for God to work on us as His masterpiece.

The Letters of Christ

By being born again we have also become the letters of Christ. This means that the Lord is writing on us all the time. The apostle Paul says this clearly in 2 Corinthians 3:3:

> *[You are] being manifested that you are a letter of Christ, cared for by us, written not with ink but with the Spirit of the living God, not on tablets of stone but on tablets of human hearts.*

Earlier, when we were considering the new life we have received, we saw that our stony hearts were replaced with hearts of flesh. Now we see that, after being born again, we experience the Lord writing on our hearts with the Spirit of the living God.

The longer we follow the Lord, the more time He has to write on us. However, it is possible for us to have been born again for a long time and yet have very little of the Lord's writing in our hearts. Yes, we are letters of Christ, but we must still allow the Lord to write on us. For example, if we desire a certain person to get saved and we pray for them, the Lord will write on us as we pray. This means there is something of Christ on our hearts that can be read, both by the Lord and by the brothers and sisters. We should tell the Lord, "Lord, now I am here to be written upon by You."

One day everything the Lord has written upon us will be manifested. Unfortunately, some believers will have "letters" that are quite short, possibly just a few sentences long. At that time, these believers will realize that their Christian life was largely wasted, for almost nothing was written on their heart. They were genuinely saved, and therefore became letters of Christ, but the Lord was not able to write very much of Himself upon them.

May the Lord be merciful to us. Every day we should say, "Lord, today I want You to write something on my heart." Our experience of the Lord is His writing on our hearts, making our letters a little longer. If we have experienced the Lord today, that means something has been written on us. Every time the Spirit moves within us and we cooperate with Him, it means the Lord is writing upon us. We need to allow the Lord to write on us throughout our entire life. Otherwise, we will surely regret the lost opportunities. May we all allow the Lord to write on us day by day throughout our lives so that we become long and substantial letters of Christ!

God's Field

In our new position, we have become God's field. First Corinthians 3:9 says,

You are God's field, God's building.

We have become God's field, His cultivated land, the ground that He tills. He works on us to make His life in us grow and produce a harvest.

God's Building

First Corinthians 3:9 also shows us that we have become God's building. God is doing something with us all the time. On the one hand, God is tilling us so that His life can grow in us, and on the other hand, God is building us together to be His corporate testimony.

God's Inheritance

The last point concerning our new position is that we have become God's inheritance. We see this in Ephesians 1:11. According to many translations, this verse is speaking of the inheritance we have in Christ. However, in some versions we see that it also refers to the fact that we have become God's inheritance. For example, in the ASV, Ephesians 1:11 says,

In [Christ] we were made a heritage, having been foreordained according to the purpose of him who worketh all things after the counsel of his will.

We, the believers, were designated as God's inheritance. However, it is only when we experience the blessings we have received in our new birth, as described in all the previous items, that God's inheritance in us can be fully realized. The apostle Paul prayed for the believers in Ephesians 1:18, asking

that the eyes of your heart may be enlightened, so that you will know what is the hope of His calling, what are the riches of the glory of His inheritance in the saints.

This shows us that God will inherit His believers. The question is, how much of us can God inherit? Some believers will have a great deal of riches for God to inherit, while other believers will have only a little. If a person was born again but never followed the Lord, God will inherit only that small part of him which was regenerated.

Enjoying Our Wonderful New Position

All of the items we have described regarding our new position are for our experience and enjoyment! The more we enjoy these riches and gain them in our experience, the more wealth there will be for God to inherit. This is not only for our own sake, but for God's inheritance. Therefore, we should pray, "Lord, we want to experience You in every aspect of our new position. We want to enjoy all the riches we received when we were born again!" Our experience of these riches will eventually become "the glory of His inheritance in the saints."

Conclusion

We have to realize that so many wonderful things happened to us the moment we believed in the Lord Jesus Christ! Formerly we were in a poor and hopeless position, but by being born again we migrated from one "country" to another. We have been transferred into an entirely new position. Now we can enjoy all of the different items that God has provided for us as a result of our being born again. We don't need to struggle to obtain them, we don't need to make up our mind and do our best to receive them, and we don't need to beg the Lord that we might enter into them, for all of these wonderful aspects of our new position belong to us

already. Every one of these points should be our joyful proc-
lamation: "I am no longer condemned, I am now justified, I
am delivered from the authority of darkness, and I am now
joined to the Lord. Praise Him!" We need to enter into the
practical enjoyment of all of these items.

The new position we have received is truly marvelous.
We should pay far more attention to our new position than
we do to our problems, failures, and limitations. In fact, if
we truly understood our position, we would forget about all
the negative things of our situation. Suppose someone were
to ask us, "Don't you still have problems, even after being
born again?" We should respond, "I don't care about my
problems. I am in the heavenlies!" Suppose they would go
on to say, "But haven't you been rebellious and disobedient
to the Lord?" We should reply, "I don't see that. I only see
that I am in resurrection." If they remind us, "Haven't you
lost your temper?" we should proclaim, "I don't know anything about that, but I do know that I am becoming God's
masterpiece."

How can we say such things? Because the Bible says them!
We believe in the word of God and not in our small failures
and defeats. We are born again, and God has transferred us
into His kingdom. May the Lord grant us the experience
and enjoyment of all the riches of our wonderful new position!

7

Our New Life Demands a New Living (1)

We have seen that being born again has three results. The moment we believed in the Lord Jesus we received a new life, a new position, and the need for a new living. Of these three results, perhaps the one that is most neglected among Christians is the third, the need for a new living.

We must realize that it is possible for us, after we are born again, to lose the practical reality of our new birth. That is, while we still have the new life within us, we may not have a new living. This does not mean that we have lost our salvation, but that we are not living according to the new life we have received. If this is our situation, then, spiritually speaking, we are just like a person lying in a hospital bed in a deep coma. No matter what you say or do, a person in a coma has no reaction. Is he still a human being? Of course. Does he have a human life? Yes. But, is he normal and healthy? No, because he has no feeling or sensation, and almost no expression. He has a human life, but not a normal human living. In the same way, it is possible for us to be born again and have God's divine life, yet not have the living that God intended for us to have when He gave us that life. Actually, when you talk with many Christians, it is clear that they are in a spiritual coma.

For example, as we indicated in the first chapter, the teaching of merely "going to heaven" can damage a believer's conscience and cause him to have no spiritual feeling or sensation. If we are born again but merely waiting to go to heaven, living however we choose, it will be difficult for others to realize that we are born again. In fact, it may even be difficult for us to realize that we are born again.

Every life demands a certain kind of living. We cannot say, "I have the human life, but I will live like a dog." That is nonsensical, for our human life demands that we have a human living. In the same way, when we were born again, we received the highest life, the very life of God, and that life within us demands that we have a living that matches God's divine life. We should not be in a "spiritual coma." Our living should match the new life we have received.

A New Living of Enjoying Christ

If we desire to live according to our new life, then we need to ask ourselves: What is the new living that we should have after being born again? The answer to this question is very simple. According to the Bible, our new living is one of enjoyment. That is, we who are born again should have a living in which we enjoy Christ day by day, and in which we constantly enjoy the riches of our salvation.

As believers in Christ, we should not consider ourselves as mere churchgoers, nor should we be satisfied with "going to heaven." If we cannot enjoy Christ today, then what is the point of hoping for the future? We should not allow ourselves to be cheated. We were born again so that we could enjoy Christ today! The Lord might say to us, "The moment you were born again I brought you into a rich enjoyment. Your living should be filled with the rich enjoyment of Me! Don't wait until the next age. Today, while you are on this earth, you should be in the rich enjoyment I prepared for you. One day the holy city, New Jerusalem, will come down out of heaven to the earth (Rev. 21:10). At that time I will display and exhibit all My riches for eternity. However, I do not want you to wait for the New Jerusalem and miss your opportunity to enjoy Me today. I want you to have a wonderful foretaste today of the New Jerusalem. I want you to enjoy all My riches in your living today."

Brought into the Enjoyment of Christ by the Spirit of Truth

How can we enter into this living of enjoying God? The Bible reveals that there is a way, and that way is the Spirit. John 16:13 begins,

> When He, the Spirit of truth, comes, He will guide you into all the truth....

In this verse, and throughout John's writings, the word "truth" does not refer simply to that which is correct or factual. Rather, it has the deeper meaning of "reality." Therefore, we may also speak of the Spirit as "the Spirit of reality." What will bring us into the reality of the enjoyment of Christ? It is the Spirit of truth, the Spirit of reality. This same verse continues,

> ...For He will not speak on His own initiative, but whatever He hears, He will speak; and He will disclose to you what is to come.

This means that the Spirit constantly unveils to us all the riches of Christ. The Spirit of truth will declare these things to us. If we are in the enjoyment of Christ, then every year we will be a different person, for we become different when the riches of this wonderful Christ are unveiled to us by the wonderful Spirit. If we want to enjoy the Lord, we must realize that all real enjoyment of Him is in the Spirit of truth.

Worshipping God, Who Is Spirit, in Our Human Spirit

How do we enter into the enjoyment of Christ, which is in the Spirit of truth? John 4:24 (NKJV) says,

God is Spirit, and those who worship Him must worship in spirit and truth.

In this verse, the Lord Jesus says something quite striking. He tells us that God is not in the physical realm, nor is He in the realm of the mind. According to the Lord Jesus, God is in the realm of the Spirit, for He is Spirit. Therefore, if we want to worship God, we need to worship Him in spirit.

We also need to realize that as God-created human beings, we have a human spirit. In fact, it is in our human spirit that we were born again. In John 3:6 the Lord Jesus Himself tells us,

That which is born of the flesh is flesh, and that which is born of the Spirit is spirit.

We were born again in our human spirit, and now we must worship God in spirit. No matter how good our mind is, we can never find God in the mental realm, because He is not in that realm. In John 4:24, Jesus is basically saying, "Do you want to know God? God is Spirit, so you must contact Him in the realm of the Spirit. Do you want to worship God? Then you must worship Him by using your human spirit."

This is not according to our natural thought. We may think that God, who is the object of our worship, has nothing to do with us. Rather, because He is so high and we are so low, we must bow down before Him. Yet, in this verse Jesus is telling us something very different. He is saying that God is Spirit, and we must worship Him in spirit. The result of such worship is that the two spirits—God the Spirit and our human spirit—become one, for genuine worship brings the Spirit and our spirit together (cf. 1 Cor. 6:17). When you worship God, who is Spirit, He is mingled with your spirit, and so you and God become one in spirit. Thus, real worship means to have a deep, personal, and intimate contact with God in spirit.

We cannot truly worship God from afar. Rather, in true worship, we become one with God. We contact Him, we experience Him, and we enjoy Him. When we worship God in spirit, it means that we enjoy all the riches of Christ. It means that the Spirit of truth operates within our spirit to unveil Christ to us for our experience and enjoyment of all that He is and desires to be to us.

Enjoying Christ as a Living Person

From all of this we see that, in our new living after being born again, we need to enjoy Christ as a living person, and this enjoyment takes place in our human spirit. The Lord doesn't want us to simply have certain kinds of moods, feelings, zeal, or excitement, nor is it His desire to simply give us physical blessings. We may desire to enjoy such things, but the Lord would tell us that such things won't last very long. The Lord wants us to enjoy Him as a living person! He would say, "I don't want to give you good feelings, excitement, or blessings. I want to give you Myself to enjoy."

Have we ever realized that we can enjoy the living Christ? Many Christians who are genuinely born again miss this enjoyment. They may enjoy God's care for them or God's blessing upon them, but few can say, "I enjoy the presence of a living person. Christ Himself is my enjoyment." We must see that Christ is a living person for us to enjoy! We are not just enjoying an emotion or a kind of excitement. We are enjoying an actual person—Christ Himself.

What kind of person is this Christ, and what are the riches of Christ that we may enjoy? Actually, the riches of Christ cannot be exhausted. In the remainder of this chapter, however, we will consider six items of His riches that are revealed in the Gospel of John.

Enjoying Christ as the Lamb of God

First, the Gospel of John tells us that Christ is the Lamb of God. John 1:29 says that John the Baptist

saw Jesus coming to him and said, "Behold, the Lamb of God who takes away the sin of the world!"

How do we enjoy Christ as the Lamb? We enjoy Him by realizing that He has taken away all our sins through His death on the cross. Our sins are not merely forgiven and covered, but taken away. This is true not only of the sins we committed yesterday, but even of the sins that we will commit twenty years from now. All our sins, past, present, and future, have already been taken away by the Lord Jesus as the Lamb of God. We should all tell the Lord, "Lord, I'm so happy. I can enjoy You as the Lamb, as my Redeemer. All my sins have been taken away. Hallelujah! There is nothing left of my sins."

We should learn to worship the Lord in this way:

Praise the Lord, I have the Lamb of God! This Lamb takes away all my sins, not only in the past, not only today, but even in the future. All my sins have been dealt with. The more I enjoy Christ, the more I feel sinless. The more I enjoy Christ, the more I'm released from the burden of sin. The more I enjoy Christ, the more I'm set apart from the world. All the negative things in the universe are taken away by my enjoyment of the Lamb of God. This is wonderful! Hallelujah!

Even when we tell the Lord, "I love You," we experience Him as the Lamb. The more we say, "Lord Jesus, I love You," and the more we take Him as a person, the more Christ as the Lamb of God becomes subjective to us. We realize, "Because of the Lamb, I'm so clean, so sanctified, and so purified. I have no more sins. I have no more problems." We don't need to pray, "Oh, Lord Jesus, take away this sin," or, "Lord Jesus, help me overcome that sin." We just need to enjoy Christ as the Lamb of God. We were born again to enjoy the living person of Christ, and this includes enjoying Him as our Lamb, the very Lamb of God. The more we enjoy this Christ—that is, the more we experience the Lamb—the more our sins are taken away.

We should have this experience all the time. On the one hand, sin is a very serious matter, and if we fall into sin we need to deal with it in a serious and thorough way. On the other hand, when we are so much in the enjoyment of the Lord's presence, we completely forget about our sins; we even forget that we are a sinner. If someone tries to tell us, "You're a sinner," we'll say, "I don't know what you mean. I don't remember that." They might say, "Didn't you behave improperly this morning?" We can respond, "Oh, I forgot all about that!" "How could you forget about that?" "I don't know. I don't think about my sins and shortcomings. I'm with Christ, the Lamb of God. This One is so holy. When I experience Him, when I enjoy Him, He takes away all the things related to sin." We should all experience such an enjoyment of Christ as the Lamb of God.

Enjoying Christ as Our Friend

We also need to enjoy Christ is as our Friend. In John 15:14 the Lord says,

You are My friends if you do what I command you.

Who is Christ? He is our Friend. This means that we can be so open with Him. When we come to the Lord, we can be honest and genuine about our situation. We don't have to hide things from Him, and we don't have to pretend. We can be completely open with Him, because He is our Friend. We can tell Him everything.

We often have the concept that the Lord is far above us, observing us, waiting for us to fall. It's as though He has a rod in His hand and is ready to punish us if we displease Him. Our thought is that if we come to His presence, His only question will be, "Have you misbehaved? Have you done anything wrong today?" Thankfully, we do not actually have such a Lord. If we did, we would all be in trouble!

Instead, Christ is our real Friend. First, He is the Lamb of God who takes away all our sins. Next, He is our Friend. The more we enjoy Christ, the more we realize that we can open up everything to Him. Even the worst sin we ever commit, we can tell Him. There may even be things that we can't tell our own family, but we can still tell Him. Because He is truly our Friend, we can talk with Him about everything. He has an ear to listen to every problem that we have, whether large or small. First Peter 5:6–7 says,

Humble yourselves under the mighty hand of God, that He may exalt you at the proper time, casting all your anxiety on Him, because He cares for you.

We can open up everything to the Lord Jesus as our Friend. I encourage you to really practice this. When you are home and have some time, try to open yourself to Him, even if it is just for a few minutes. Tell Him everything. Tell Him even about all the things that you think are too shameful, too low, or too insignificant to speak of. You may feel that there are some things you cannot tell Him, but that is not true. The more you are aware of such things, the more you should let Him know all about them. You should tell the Lord, "Lord, I'm thankful that You are my Friend, and I can tell You everything. Lord, let me tell You about all my problems. Let me tell You about all my frustrations."

Only you know what your real problems are. If you say that you have no problems, then you must be God Himself. If you are not God, then surely you have problems and anxieties in your daily life. So what can you do? You should learn to enjoy Christ as a living person by opening your whole being to Him with all of your problems. He is your Friend, and He will listen to you. He knows, He understands, and He can fellowship with you and restore you.

Enjoying Christ as the Firstborn Son of God

We should also enjoy Christ as the firstborn Son of God. In John 20:17 He told Mary, on the day He was resurrected,

Go to My brethren and say to them, "I ascend to My Father and your Father, and My God and your God."

When Christ was resurrected, He was declared the first-born Son of God, and at the same time we became His many brothers (Rom. 1:4; 8:29). To understand this, we must realize that as God, Christ was eternally the Son of God (John 17:5), but as a man He shared in our created human nature (Luke 1:31; Col. 1:15). Through His resurrection He was glorified and exalted as a man, and hence as a man declared to be the Son of God. As such a one, He is now "the first-born among many brothers" (Rom. 8:29–30). Therefore, to say that the Lord is the Firstborn means that He is the pioneering One. Through His death and resurrection He uplifted the human nature, and now we need to follow Him by going through that same process. That is, our human nature is also being uplifted as we experience the cross (Rom. 6:4) and partake of the divine nature (2 Pet. 1:4). In this way, we will become the many sons of God, the many brothers of Christ, the firstborn son of God.

This glorification of Christ as the Firstborn Son also means that we will become the same as He is. We are being conformed to His image. In other words, He is the pattern for what we are becoming. Someday we will all be exactly the same as this wonderful Christ is today (1 John 3:1–2).

Enjoying Christ as the Good Shepherd

We should enjoy Christ as our good Shepherd. The Lord says in John 10:11,

I am the good shepherd; the good shepherd lays down His life for the sheep.

And in John 10:14 He says,

I am the good shepherd, and I know My own and My own know Me.

When He was on the earth, the Lord shepherded us to the extent that He even laid down His life for us on the cross. Now He is our good Shepherd, even our great Shepherd (Heb. 13:20), in the heavenly places. He has ascended and is enthroned with authority, kingship, and lordship. As such a One, He is shepherding us today. He shepherds us outwardly by sovereignly arranging our lives, and He shepherds us inwardly by ministering Himself to us in the midst of our situations. We don't have to fear or worry about His care for us, because Christ is the good Shepherd.

Our enjoyment of Christ as our Shepherd should bring us peace. We don't need to be so anxious or concerned about the different things in our lives, and we don't need to worry so much about our future, our marriage, our job, or our education. The Lord is on the throne, and there is no need to worry. He is our good Shepherd. If we know such a wonderful Christ, we will truly worship Him. We can pray,

Lord, I worship You for being such a great and wonderful Shepherd! My life is in Your hands, and I can entrust myself to You.

Enjoying Christ as the Builder of His Body

We should also enjoy Christ as the Builder of the body of Christ. In John 2:19 Jesus declared to the Jews,

Destroy this temple, and in three days I will raise it up.

The temple the Lord is speaking of in this verse is not the physical temple in Jerusalem, but the temple of His body. What is the Lord building today? He is building the temple of His mystical body. Christ was resurrected with a physical body. Then in resurrection, the Lord as the Spirit was imparted into us. Now all of us are His body, the mystical body of Christ.

When Simon declared that the Lord Jesus was "the Christ, the Son of the Living God" (Matt. 16:16) the Lord replied, in Matthew 16:18,

> *I also say to you that you are Peter, and upon this rock I will build My church; and the gates of Hades will not overpower it.*

Later, in his first letter to his fellow believers, this same Peter said that we are all "living stones" who are being built up to be God's house (1 Pet. 2:5). The apostle Paul spoke of the Lord's building work by saying that we are members of His body, and that this body is building itself up in love (Eph. 5:30, 4:16). From all this we see that we are now the building materials for the Lord to build us up together as His body. Thus, we should not have an individualistic Christian life. The more we enjoy the Lord, the more we will be built up as the body of Christ.

The building up of the body cannot be carried out by our human effort. It is not a matter of saying to each other, "I want to be built up with you." Although it may be good to say this, if we really want to be built up together, we should simply enjoy the person of Christ. He is the Builder of His body, and the more we enjoy Him as a living person in our spirit, the more we will be built up into the body of Christ. The more we labor on Christ, enjoy the person of Christ, and spend time in the presence of Christ, the more we will be one with all the other members of the body, because the building of the body of Christ takes place through our enjoyment of the Builder Himself. We don't have to make up our mind and struggle to be built up. As we enjoy the living person of Christ, the Builder of the body, we will automatically be built up with all the other members of His body.

Enjoying Christ as the Bridegroom

We also need to enjoy Christ as our dear Bridegroom. John 3:29 quotes John the Baptist. He said,

He who has the bride is the bridegroom; but the friend of the bridegroom, who stands and hears him, rejoices greatly because of the bridegroom's voice. So this joy of mine has been made full.

Here, John the Baptist calls himself "the friend of the bridegroom." As the friend, he rejoiced that Christ, the Bridegroom, was gaining a bride. We, the believers, are this bride. As we are being built up as the body, we are also being prepared to be His bride to marry Him.

The more we enjoy the living person of Christ, the more we will have the sense that we are being betrothed to Him. When we are spending time in the Lord's presence, we may begin to pray, "Oh Lord Jesus, I love You. Oh Lord, I love You so much! I just want to give You my whole being. Oh Lord Jesus, I belong to You. You are so satisfying. You are so nourishing. You are so strengthening. You are so wonderful, so fresh, and so sweet." When we pray in such a way, we will surely feel, "I'm going to marry this One. I'm going to marry this wonderful Bridegroom, Jesus Christ. Hallelujah!" By enjoying the Lord Jesus as a living person in our spirit, we are being prepared to marry Him.

Conclusion

We need to have a deep realization that God is Spirit, and thus if we want to worship Him, we must worship Him in spirit. The Spirit we enjoy is the Spirit of truth, who is bringing us into all the reality of what God is (John 16:13). He is also unveiling all the riches of Christ to us, which are in our spirit, where there is no ritual, form, or religious practice. In our spirit we enjoy a living person.

How do we enjoy this Christ? We enjoy Him as the Lamb; all our sins are taken away. We enjoy Him as our Friend; we can tell Him all our problems. We enjoy Him as our older Brother; we are going to be the same as He is. We enjoy Him as the good Shepherd; He is the trustworthy, sovereign One who arranges every step of our lives. We enjoy Him as the Builder; He is building us into His body and into the practical church life. And we enjoy Him as our Bridegroom; we are going to marry Him. Oh, we have such a wonderful Christ!

The more we fellowship over these points, the more our spirits will be stirred up. Our Christ is so lovely, so enjoyable, and so real! He is our Lamb, our Friend, our older Brother, our Shepherd, our Builder, and our Bridegroom! When we enjoy Him in this way, we realize that we have no more problems and no more difficulties. We don't have to make any effort to do anything, for we were not born again so that we would have to struggle so hard. Rather, we were born again into a living of enjoyment, a living in which we daily enjoy Christ as everything to us. We worship the Lord for this. May we all tell the Lord how much we love Him and enjoy Him!

I love You, Lord! In the whole universe I don't want to care for anyone or anything else. I only want to care for You. Lord, may You gain me completely for

Yourself. Thank You for all that You are to me! Thank You that I can know You and enjoy You as such a wonderful living person!

8

Our New Life Demands a New Living (2)

We have seen that being born again results in the need for a new living, one of enjoying Christ as a living person. We should enjoy Christ as the Lamb, as our Friend, as our older Brother, as our Shepherd, as the Builder, and as our Bridegroom. The more we enjoy Him, the more we have the reality of all these items. We will be cleansed, sustained, and strengthened, and we will have the living and subjective experience of Christ in our daily life. When we enjoy Christ, we are actually giving God the worship He desires, because to God, the true worship is the enjoyment of Christ. This enjoyment takes place in our human spirit, where the Spirit of reality unveils all the riches of Christ to us.

Enjoying Christ as the Supply for Our Daily Needs

Now we will cover several more aspects of the riches of Christ in the Gospel of John. In this chapter, we want to consider a number of items that focus on Christ being the supply to meet our daily needs. In the Gospel of John, we see that Christ is life to us. He is the bread of life, the water of life, the light of life, and the word of life. He is also grace, reality, satisfaction, and freedom. He is also the resurrection, and He is the true vine. The enjoyment of all these riches will supply us to meet all the needs in our daily life.

Enjoying Christ as Life

Our first need as Christians is to enjoy the life of Christ, for if we don't enjoy Christ as our life, then we can't have Him as anything else in our experience. It is only when we enjoy Christ as life that we will be able to experience Him as all the other items He is to us.

Moreover, if we are short of the enjoyment of Christ as our life, in our experience everything will become gloomy, and nothing of Christ will be appealing to us. We will tell the Lord, "Lord, I know so many things about You, but they are not real to me. I know that you are my Lord and that You take care of me, but I don't really feel anything. I know that You are 'all in all' and that I should be joyful, but I cannot be joyful."

Have we ever had this experience? Many times we know what should be true in our Christian life, but it is not real to us. We know that as Christians we should be dynamic, powerful, and energetic. We know we should be joyful, cheerful, and excited. We know all these things, but we just can't be these things. Why aren't we able to be what we know we're supposed to be? It is because we are short of the enjoyment of Christ as life. Only Christ as life can meet our daily needs.

Suppose we wake up in the morning and simply feel down. There's no need to remain in such a state, and we don't need to condemn ourselves, saying, "Oh, I'm so poor. I'm so weak." We just need to turn to the Lord and enjoy Christ as life. We should open the Bible and begin to call on the Lord's name, even just a little (cf. Rom. 10:12–13 and 1 Cor. 12:3).

We can call out from deep within our spirit, "Oh, Lord Jesus. Oh, Lord Jesus." We can turn to the Bible and read one verse, and then call on the Lord again and pray for just a little while. Then we can read another verse and pray again, just a little. It doesn't need to be long, perhaps just ten or twenty minutes, but soon we will be filled with Christ as our life. We will feel that our sleepiness is gone, our bad feeling is gone, our depression is gone, our problems and our anxieties are gone, and that everything negative is gone. Why is this? Because we are enjoying Christ as our very life. Suddenly, we will be full of a desire to love and serve the Lord and to spend more time with our brothers and sisters in the church. The more we come to the Lord in this way, the more we will find a tide of life rising up within us.

There is a great secret to the Christian life, which is simply this: we should never abide in our problems, and we should never condemn ourselves. As those who are born again, we are often overly sensitive. If anything is wrong with our spiritual condition, we know it immediately, and we feel it intensely. When something is improper in our lives, such as a sin, or a love for the world, we are deeply troubled by it. While there are times when we need to deal with such things in a serious way, we should not focus on such problems, nor should we condemn ourselves. Rather, we should immediately turn to enjoy Christ as our life. If the world is overpowering us, we should turn to enjoy Christ as life. If we are aware of something sinful or unhealthy in our life, we should turn to enjoy Christ as our life. The more Satan tries to upset our environment, the more we should enjoy Christ as our life. Christ as our life is the answer! He is the supply to meet our needs. We should be able to say, "The life of Christ is nourishing me, strengthening me, supporting me, and enlightening me. I have all I need in His life!"

A person who is religious or ethical never feels the need to enjoy the life of Christ, for he is satisfied with trying to improve himself and trying to behave properly. But we who are born again have received the need for a new living, a living in which we enjoy and even depend on the life of Christ. We should say, "I don't want a sinful life, I don't want an ethical life, I don't want a worldly life, and I don't want a religious life. I want a life that comes from the enjoyment of Christ Himself as my life!"

Enjoying Christ as the Bread of Life

The enjoyment of Christ as life is very good and very necessary, but it is also somewhat general. In addition to enjoying Christ as our life, we should also enjoy Him as all the items we need day by day for our spiritual living. We can begin by eating Him as our bread of life, to be the strength for our daily living. In John 6:35 and 57, Jesus says,

I am the bread of life; he who comes to Me will not hunger, and he who believes in Me will never thirst....As the living Father sent Me, and I live because of the Father, so he who eats Me, he also will live because of Me.

It is by eating Christ as the bread of life that we are constantly made alive. Whenever we eat the bread of life, we live because of Him.

Enjoying Christ as the Water of Life

We also need to enjoy Christ as the water of life to quench our thirst. John 7:37–38 says,

*Now on the last day, the great day of the feast, Jesus
stood and cried out, saying, "If anyone is thirsty, let
him come to Me and drink. He who believes in Me,
as the Scripture said, 'From his innermost being will
flow rivers of living water.'"*

In our human life, we need to eat, and we also need to
drink. This means we need to be strengthened, and we also
need to be refreshed. No matter how much we enjoy Christ
as the bread of life, we also need Him as the water of life.

In our Christian life, it is possible to be made alive and
strengthened and yet still be thirsty. We need something that
can refresh us. We need to drink something for our thirst to
be quenched. The world has many kinds of "drinks" to
quench our thirst, but as the Lord said, if we drink of these
things we will thirst again (John 4:13). However, when we
drink Christ Himself as the water of life we are refreshed,
and our thirst is truly quenched (John 4:14).

Enjoying Christ as the Light of Life

We also need to enjoy Christ as the Light of life. In John
8:12 Jesus says,

*I am the Light of the world; he who follows Me will
not walk in the darkness, but will have the Light of
life.*

When we enjoy Christ as the Light of life, we are no longer
in darkness. We know how to walk properly, and we realize
what is right and what is wrong. Christ as the Light of life
shines within us for our daily walk.

Enjoying Christ
as the Word of Life

We also need to enjoy Christ as the word of life. The Lord Jesus said, in John 5:39–40,

> *You search the Scriptures because you think that in them you have eternal life; it is these that testify about Me; and you are unwilling to come to Me so that you may have life.*

Then later He added, in John 6:63,

> *It is the Spirit who gives life; the flesh profits nothing; the words that I have spoken to you are spirit and are life.*

This means that the Bible itself is the word of life for us to enjoy. We should not think that it is just a book for us to study, for that is too objective. When we say that the Bible is the word of life, we mean that it is very subjective to us. It is a shame that so many Christians take the Bible merely as a book of ethics and teachings, and not as a book of life. They simply don't know the riches of Christ that are in the word! If we only search the Bible for ethical teachings, we are looking for the wrong thing. Every word in the Bible is a word of life, because the purpose of the Bible is to give us Christ Himself for us to enjoy as the word of life. This enjoyment energizes us to follow Him.

In whatever way we enjoy the Lord—by praying, praising, singing a song, reading the word, or in any other way—what we receive is life. The life we enjoy has several aspects: the bread of life to make us alive and strengthen us, the water of life to quench our thirst and refresh us, the light of life to shine for our daily walk, and the word of life to energize us. This is wonderful! Praise the Lord that we can enjoy Him as life, the One with all of these riches to meet our daily needs!

Enjoying Christ as Grace

In addition to experiencing Christ as life, we should also experience Him as grace. John 1:14 says,

The Word became flesh, and dwelt among us, and we saw His glory, glory as of the only begotten from the Father, full of grace and truth.

As Christians we often ask the Lord for His grace, yet, do we actually realize what grace is? In these messages we have spoken a great deal concerning the enjoyment of Christ. Now we need to realize that this enjoyment is grace. That is, grace is simply the enjoyment of Christ.

The Lord is full of grace for us to enjoy. Unfortunately, we often misunderstand God and assume He is angry with us. We may even tell the Lord, "Lord, I did something wrong again. Please don't punish me too much." Actually, we should realize that the Lord is not out to punish us, and He doesn't have a harsh countenance towards us. Rather, His countenance towards us is always pleasant, expressing His desire that we would enjoy Him as grace.

We should learn to enjoy this grace, and not just the blessings we receive from Christ. The problem is that many Christians develop a taste for outward blessings and never desire the Giver Himself. They don't really desire Christ, but they want all kinds of gifts from Christ. That is why their Christian lives are so poor. We need to realize that the Lord loves us and is full of grace towards us, desiring that we would enjoy Himself as grace. If we receive His grace in this way, our Christian lives will become very prevailing.

Enjoying Christ
as Reality

John 1:14 says that Christ is "full of grace and truth." As we have already stressed, throughout John's writings the word "truth" means more than just "correct"; it has the meaning of "reality." Therefore, this verse means that when we enjoy Christ as grace, we also have Him as reality.

Without Christ as reality, our life is empty, but if we have Christ as reality, we will not desire anything else. We will realize that everything else is false, and everything else is vain. The only reality in this universe is Christ Himself. We must enjoy, experience, and substantiate this Christ as the only One who is real! When Christ is genuinely experienced by us, that is reality. The more we have Christ as grace, the more we have Him as reality.

Enjoying Christ
as Satisfaction

After we experience Christ as grace and reality, we will have Him as our satisfaction. The story of the Lord changing the water into wine at the wedding feast in Cana is quite well-known. After this miracle, the master of the feast told the bridegroom, in John 2:10,

Every man serves the good wine first, and when the people have drunk freely, then he serves the poorer wine; but you have kept the good wine until now.

The Lord, who is the "good wine," is better than all the wine, or satisfaction, the world can offer. Christ Himself is the highest satisfaction. Nothing in the world compares to Him.

Enjoying Christ
as Freedom

Christ is also the true freedom. In John 8:32 and 36, the Lord says,

You will know the truth, and the truth will make you free....So if the Son makes you free, you will be free indeed.

How can the truth make us free? This truth is not a matter of knowing things doctrinally. Doctrinal knowledge can never set us free. It is when we enjoy Christ as grace, reality, and satisfaction that we are set free. When we have Christ as our freedom, neither sin, nor the world, nor anything negative can bind us. When we enjoy Christ, we can say, "I have the truth. I have the Son. I'm free!"

Enjoying Christ
as the Resurrection

We should also enjoy Christ as the resurrection. Jesus says in John 11:25,

I am the resurrection and the life; he who believes in Me will live even if he dies.

Because Jesus Himself is the resurrection, those who enjoy Him as life will also be in the reality of resurrection. When we enjoy Christ as the resurrection life, we reign over everything. We reign over the small things, such as our concerns for our appearance, and we reign over the big things, such as our concerns for the future. We reign over all our problems, anxieties, and situations. When we are in resurrection, we don't care for anything else. Thus, we need to be in resurrection so that we can live an overcoming Christian life, a life in which we reign over everything.

Enjoying Christ as the True Vine

Finally, we should enjoy Christ as the true vine. In John 15:1 the Lord says,

I am the true vine, and My Father is the vinedresser.

This is a famous verse, but very few understand it. Christ is not only the vine itself; He is also the very life of the vine. There is an organic union between us, who are the branches within the vine, and Christ, who is the life of the vine.

The Lord goes on to say, in John 15:5,

I am the vine, you are the branches; he who abides in Me and I in him, he bears much fruit, for apart from Me you can do nothing.

When we were born again, we received the life of the vine and became part of that vine. Now we are one with Christ as the branches in the true vine, and thus receive the life of the vine and express all the riches of the vine.

Although it is often neglected, one aspect of our need

for a new living is this need to live as members of the body of Christ. However, if we realize that we are branches in the vine, it will very much help us to see the corporate aspect of our new birth, for the vine is a corporate matter. We were not just born again as individuals, for in the vine, there are many branches. The more we enjoy Christ in all His riches for our daily life, the more we become part of the corporate expression of the body of Christ. This is to enjoy Christ as the true vine.

We will cover this matter of the corporate aspect of our new life more thoroughly in the final chapter.

9

Our New Life Demands a New Living (3)

We have seen that when we were born again we received the need for a new living. This new living has two aspects. The first aspect, which we have covered, is the enjoyment of Christ. The second aspect, which will be the focus of this chapter, is that this new living is for the body of Christ and the practical church life.

These two aspects of our new living are closely related. Ultimately, we can only have the enjoyment of Christ in the body of Christ, and it is our enjoyment of Christ which, in turn, makes us a blessing to the body of Christ. We may even say that all of our enjoyment of Christ is really for the body of Christ.

A New Living for the Body of Christ

As we have seen, the life that we received when we were born again demands that we have a corporate living. We can no longer be individualistic, for when we were born again we were born into the body of Christ.

Unfortunately, Americans are raised in a culture that is very individualistic, which always tells you to "be yourself."

In this country everyone is encouraged from childhood to do whatever they like so that they can find self-fulfillment. They are told that whatever they consider to be right or whatever they want to do, they should just do. But now, after being born again, everything is different. We can no longer live by ourselves, for we have been born into the body of Christ to live the corporate "body life."

This new life in the body of Christ can be demonstrated by looking at our own physical body. When we look at our physical body, we realize that God is truly wise. Only He could put things together in such a wonderful way, so perfect in every detail. Every part of our body is fully coordinated with every other part. Every member has its particular function, yet all the members function together as one body.

In the body of Christ, we see God's wisdom in an even greater way than in the human body. Now that we are born again, we can no longer remain as isolated individuals, for we have received the need for a new living, a corporate living in which we are the members of the body of Christ and in which we function in harmony with all the other members of this body. Where do we experience this in a practical way? In the local church life.

The Lord's Three Commissions for Us in the Body of Christ

In considering our new living, we have so far focused on the enjoyment of Christ in its different aspects, especially in the Gospel of John. Now we want to go on to see how, in this new living, the Lord requires something from us, for our being born again does involve some responsibility. In doing so, we will once again consider the Gospel of John, for this book reveals that Christ has three commissions for us. As we consider these commissions, we can see that since we are in the body of Christ, we should not focus only on ourselves, but also care for others. However, we should not view this as a heavy requirement. Rather, we should consider it as the sum of our enjoyment of all the riches of Christ that we have covered previously.

Our First Commission:
To Love One Another

The first commission the Lord gave us is to love one another. He says in John 15:12,

This is My commandment, that you love one another,
just as I have loved you.

We should love one another as Christ first loved us. We must be careful, however, that our love is genuine. Our love should not be a natural love, one that involves self-interest. We may feel that if I do something for you, and you do something for me, it means we love each other. However, that is actually a degraded, political kind of love, a love that merely involves the exchanging of favors. The love that exists among us should be a love that imparts life into one another, even as Christ loved us by dying for us and then imparting His life into us.

We need to love one another in the body of Christ, to the point that, as the Lord did for us, we would forsake our lives for our fellow believers. We should learn to lay down our lives for the sake of our brothers and sisters by being absolutely poured out for their sake. We should also learn how to impart the divine life into the saints. This is what it truly means to love one another according to the first commission the Lord gave to us.

Our Second Commission:
To Keep the Oneness

Second, the Lord commissioned us to keep the oneness with our fellow believers. He prayed to the Father, in John 17:11 and 21,

Holy Father, keep them in Your name, the name which You have given Me, that they may be one even as We are....That they may all be one; even as You, Father, are in Me and I in You, that they also may be in Us, so that the world may believe that You sent Me.

This commission of keeping the oneness is closely related to the first commission of loving one another. If we love one another as Christ has loved us, then in such a love we will be able to keep the oneness.

Why is the body of Christ so divided today? Because there is a shortage of this kind of love. Christians often love their doctrines and practices more than they love their brothers and sisters. They would say, "I love the doctrines I believe, and you love the doctrines you believe. I love the practices I have, and you love the practices you have." They don't realize that our new life should cause us to be poured out, not upon these things, but upon our brothers and sisters.

As those who have been born again to become the members of the body of Christ, we should learn to enjoy the Lord's life and grace together, and then we should love one another. This means that we should impart life to one another and pour ourselves out upon our fellow believers.

In such a love, we must endeavor to keep the oneness. We should not fight for practices or argue about doctrines, for neither of these is what really matters. What we do need is to be one. Among us there should be such a treasure, namely, that we love each other and that we are one. We shouldn't care about anything except loving one another and keeping the oneness of the body of Christ.

Our Third Commission: To Feed and Shepherd Our Fellow Believers

The third and final commission from Christ in the Gospel of John is found in 21:15–17. That commission is to "feed My lambs," "shepherd My sheep," and "feed My sheep" (Darby). From the moment we are born again, we should learn how to feed and shepherd someone. No one is too young in the Christian life to learn this. Often, we think that our problem is our self, but the real problem is that we don't have a lamb to care for. Don't say, "I was just recently saved. How can I care for anyone else? I'm the one who needs feeding and shepherding." If we are young in the Lord, then as one young lamb we can care for another young lamb. Surely there are some lambs in our local church for us to feed.

Conclusion

We need to say, "Lord, I'm so thankful that I can enjoy You as life. Now the life within me demands a new living. I realize that You have brought me into the body of Christ and have given me three commissions. Lord, I want to be faithful to Your three commissions." What are these commissions? First, we should love one another and give ourselves to one another. Second, we should keep the oneness and not care for doctrines and practices. And third, we should feed and shepherd someone. We all have to learn how to feed and shepherd our fellow believers.

We were born again into the body of Christ. Therefore,

we should no longer be by ourselves, nor should we just care for ourselves. Rather, we should love one another, we should keep the oneness, and we should feed and shepherd the lambs and the sheep. These are the three commissions for us in the Gospel of John. May the Lord be merciful to us!

Thank You, Lord, that we are born again. Now we want to enjoy and carry out Your commissions. We want to live the body life by enjoying You as life and grace. We are not here for ourselves; we are here for Your interest. Strengthen us to carry out these commissions! We give ourselves to You, that we would love one another, keep the oneness, and feed Your lambs. Thank You, Lord Jesus, for these three commissions!

Online Ministry by Titus Chu

MinistryMessages.org is the online archive for the ministry of Titus Chu. This includes audio messages, articles, and books in PDF format, all of which are available as free downloads.

The online *Fellowship Journal* is also carried now on MinistryMessages.org. Each month, it features a single article taken from Titus' recent ministry.

"Daily Words for the Christian Life" is an e-letter sent out every Thursday. It features selections from the writings of Titus Chu. To subscribe, visit MinistryMessages.org/subscribe.

Books by Titus Chu

The books listed below are available in print, Kindle, and iBook format, in addition to the free PDF editions offered on our website. Go to MinistryMessages.org/order to see the full listing, or search for them directly on Amazon.com and iTunes.

Born Again: Our New Life in Christ

Born Again: The Study Guide

David: After God's Heart

Elijah & Elisha: Living for God's Testimony

Ruth: Growth unto Maturity

Philippians: That I May Gain Christ

A Sketch of Genesis

Two Manners of Life

Made in the USA
Columbia, SC
10 June 2019